What Readers Say About

This study is refreshing for the soul! Dr. Scott gives married couples practical tools for strengthening your relationship with God, together. As a working newlywed myself, I appreciate Dr. Scott's openness to the struggles of marriage. She makes getting to know your spouse easy!

~ Chelcie Ospino

Reading through the text of *Just You, Me and God*, by week three we knew this was a study we were eager to start together. This guide through the Bible touches a need most couples don't even recognize they have: to know and understand how each thinks about and lives out faith. From this inspiring start, *Just You, Me and God* nudges a year-long discussion that answers the question: what are we doing with Jesus today? Engaging, thoughtful and surprising, *Just You, Me and God* redefines date night.

~ Rev. Steve Grove, BTh, MTS, DMin (candidate), Senior Pastor Louise Street Community Church;
~ Bonnie Grove, best-selling author of *Your Best You: Discovering and Developing Strengths God Gave You*

Latayne's discernment in amalgamating God's commandments and Christ's teachings and examples on earth is the major theme in *Just You, Me and God*. Spouses will learn how to study both Old Testament and New Testament scriptures to utilize God's love, commands, principles and blessings in their marriages.

~ Denise Keefe

Just You, Me and God—a great title for a wonderful tool to grow in your knowledge of God and His will.

~ Donna Watson

A wonderful guide for married couples to use for years to come! There is no greater life and marriage strengthener than couples frequently praying and reading/discussing the Bible together. This is what God intends for His children in marriage. Dive in!

~ Lt. Col. Dave Leaumont, MDiv

I want to thank Latayne for writing this book! It fills a gap that my husband and I have felt, but which, for some reason, we have never thought to try to fill. We've felt the need for unity in our readings and tried many times, with differing amounts of success, to read the Bible together regularly. Unfortunately, this often means reading in the evenings when we are both tired and not in great mental shape to generate much discussion. The format of this devotional allows us to read whenever we need to, while still filling that need for unity in the weekly discussion. It also provides some wonderful background and direction to begin the discussion, and the commonplacing element facilitates our individual preparation for when we come together. In other words, this is just what we didn't know we needed. I believe this will become a well-loved tool in our endeavor to create and maintain a family culture that is rooted in Christ.

~ Carreen Raynor

As we began our life as a married couple, we received this beautiful book. Through its pages we grew into two becoming one, submitting to the One. *Just You, Me and God* is a gem for any couple in any part of their journey.

~ Celeste Green, Academic Dean, Oak Grove Classical Academy

JUST YOU, ME AND GOD

A Devotional Guide for Couples
Reading Through the Bible in One Year

by
Latayne C. Scott, PhD.

TRINITY SOUTHWEST UNIVERSITY PRESS
Albuquerque, New Mexico

TRINITY SOUTHWEST UNIVERSITY PRESS
Albuquerque, NM

Copyright © 2016 by Latayne C. Scott
ISBN: 978-1-945750-04-5

Other books in the Doorway Documents collection:

Passion, Power, Proxy, Release: Scriptures, Poems, and Devotional Thoughts for Communion and Worship Services by Latayne C. Scott, Ph.D.

The Heart's Door: Hospitality in the Bible by Latayne C. Scott, Ph.D.

Cover design by Noel Green, Park East Inc.

Just You, Me and God
is dedicated with great love
to Dennis and Elayne Snyder,
faithful patrons and examples of generosity

This book is produced by the generosity of patrons of Latayne C. Scott.

For more information, go to www.patreon.com/Latayne

Acknowledgments

I gratefully salute Sharon K. Souza and Phil Silvia for their fine editing and other contributions to the layout of this book. Dr. J. Michael Strawn, Celeste Green, and others gave valuable input.

Introduction

This guide will help you study through God's Word in one year's time. It will also provide a common spiritual reference point for you both.

You are strongly encouraged to select one evening a week to spend alone with one another. This will be hard at first, but people you know will come to respect you for the importance and priority you place on your marriage. If you have children and can afford it, select a babysitter who can sit for your children for a couple of hours a week on a regular basis. If you cannot afford it, there is probably another couple who would be willing to trade babysitting with you. If this is not possible, check with your congregation's youth leader to see if any teenagers would be willing to rotate sitting for you as a service project. Exhaust all possibilities among friends and relatives: Your time together is essential for the health of your souls and your marriage.

Both husband and wife will be reading the same Bible passages daily. It is not necessary that you both read together. Some people find it helpful to read the Old Testament passages in the morning and the New Testament passages at night. Others read the whole day's readings at one sitting. Each should have his or her own Bible, preferably a modern version with easy-to-read print, and each should mark passages that have special meaning or about which he or she might have questions. (Small "sticky notes" are a helpful, temporary way to mark such passages.) You might research questions that come up by consulting reliable commentaries, or asking a minister or other mature Christian. Good commentaries would also be helpful for background materials, especially on Old Testament prophets and New Testament epistles.

• Your book contains blank pages along with each week's readings. This is a place to make some notes about questions you might have regarding certain passages, or to jot down a "new" or "old" favorite scripture. This practice of *"commonplacing,"* or writing significant quotations down in a separate book, is an ancient and beloved help to many readers through the ages.

- Your discussion time each week with your spouse will be "open book"—a time to talk over passages of interest, and to answer together the questions in this devotional guide. There are not necessarily "right" and "wrong" answers to these questions in many cases. They are designed to stimulate discussion, not to answer deep theological questions. Each partner is free to share insights gained from his or her own study and experience.

- Of particular interest to students of Representational Research are the questions about generalizations at the end of each study.

What's a generalization? A generalization is a principle extracted from a particular scriptural passage or group of scriptural passages. It's something that is exemplified in those passages, but also is a principle that is true throughout the Bible.

For example, the story of David against Goliath might produce this generalization: No physical factor is determinative when the will of God is operating.

That generalization can then be applied to other similar experiences that you might face. How would you use this generalization in your own life? You might think of a physical factor (finances or illness, for instance), and write out how that physical factor can't determine anything in your life if the will of God—or His promises—oppose it.

The generalizations you will be asked to formulate will be those concerning the character and actions of God. For instance, we might generalize from the story of the Creation: God is orderly and methodical and extravagant in dealing with the world He created.

Notice that neither of the generalizations above are applications; they are rather the principles on which you would subsequently make an application to a particular situation or condition in your own life.

- **The "focus" scriptures for each week are scriptures of special interest. They can be used for memory work, if you desire. And don't forget to pray together!**

It may sound like a lot of work—setting aside a certain night each week turning down other invitations, getting a babysitter, finding time to read God's Word daily.

But what results you'll reap!

You will have a common reference point on spiritual things.

Your children will see your priorities, and you'll have gems of biblical insight to share with them. "Teach them to your children," Deuteronomy 11:19 says. "Talk about them when you are at home and when you are on the road, when you are going to bed and when you are getting up."

Your spouse, your children, and your family will have a closeness to God and to each other that can't be gained any other way!

WEEK 1

How exciting to begin this journey together, to strengthen your marriage and have a "common ground" of spiritual growth while you learn about our God and His Word!

DATE WE BEGAN:

Old Testament/New Testament
- o   Day 1   Genesis 1-3/Matthew 1
- o   Day 2   Genesis 4-6/Matthew 2
- o   Day 3   Genesis 7-9/Matthew 3
- o   Day 4   Genesis 10-12/Matthew 4
- o   Day 5   Genesis 13-15/Matthew 5:1-26
- o   Day 6   Genesis 16-17/Matthew 5:27-48
- o   Day 7   Genesis 18-19/Matthew 6:1-18

Focus scripture: Gen. 15:6/Matthew 5:43-48

QUESTIONS

1.   What characteristics of God have you seen in the way that He dealt with His people in Genesis chapters 1-19? List some.

2. What shows you that He is a God who listens to the opinions and is attentive to the individual needs of those who love Him? Are there some examples from our readings of how He spoke to some people and then listened to them when they had a conflicting view on something?

3. Who quoted scripture at the temptation of Jesus? What does this tell you about how scripture can be used and misused? How are the three things Satan offered Jesus tempting to you? How do you overcome such temptation?

4. Look through the Sermon on the Mount and tell how at least one principle taught there helped you this past week (or could have been of help if you'd thought of it at the time.)

5. What could you generalize about the way God relates to people and/or human circumstances from any of this week's readings? (You might want to refer back to Question 1 to jump-start some of your thinking, and the example given in this book's Introduction.)

SCRIPTURES I WANT TO REMEMBER
AND ADDITIONAL NOTES

Gen 3:21

WEEK 2

Old Testament/New Testament
- Day 1   Genesis 20-22/Matthew 6:19-34
- Day 2   Genesis 23-24/Matthew 7
- Day 3   Genesis 25-26/Matthew 8:1-17
- Day 4   Genesis 27-28/Matthew 8:18-34
- Day 5   Genesis 29-30/Matthew 9:1-17
- Day 6   Genesis 31-32/Matthew 9:18-38
- Day 7   Genesis 33-35/Matthew 10:1-20

Focus scripture: Genesis 22:14/Matthew 7:7-11.

QUESTIONS

1. There is a lot of history covered in Genesis chapters 20 through 35, but three themes seem to stand out: sacrifice, rivalry, and married love.

   a. How did the following people sacrifice something important, and what were the results: Abraham? Esau? Jacob?

   b. Give examples of rivalry from these chapters. Was the rivalry in any case a healthy or good thing? Did it ever have good results? Did it frustrate the intentions or plans of God for His people?

c. Look at examples of married love found in these chapters. How can these models of married love at their best help your marriage?

2. Jesus said in Matthew 6:25-34 not to worry about our needs, for God knows them and will take care of them. Then later in Matthew 7:7-11 He urged us to ask for what we needed from God. How do you reconcile these two statements? In what way do you put both into practice?

3. Look at the miracles in this week's readings from the New Testament. What part did faith play in each? In which cases was the faith not of the one who was healed?

4. What could you generalize about the way God relates to people and/or human circumstances from any of this week's readings?

SCRIPTURES I WANT TO REMEMBER
AND ADDITIONAL NOTES

WEEK 3

Old Testament/New Testament

- o   Day 1   Genesis 36-38/Matthew 10:31-42
- o   Day 2   Genesis 39-40/Matthew 11
- o   Day 3   Genesis 41-42/Matthew 12:1-23
- o   Day 4   Genesis 43-45/Matthew 12:24-50
- o   Day 5   Genesis 46-48/Matthew 13:1-30
- o   Day 6   Genesis 49-50/Matthew 13:31-58
- o   Day 7   Exodus 1-3/Matthew 14:1-21

Focus scripture: Genesis 29:20/Matthew 10:28-31

QUESTIONS

1. List the times in his life that Joseph could have given up on ever being "successful" in life.

2. In chapters 49 and 50 of Genesis, what ways did Joseph say that God had worked ahead of time to provide food for His people? What did Joseph say about how God overpowered even people's evil intentions in order to accomplish His goals? Does He work in a similar way today in your lives? Can you give examples?

3. When John the Baptist was in prison, he sent his disciples to Jesus to ask if He was the Messiah. How did Jesus answer? How can looking at Jesus' power (as manifested in His works) help you when you are in trouble?

4. Look at various teaching methods used by Jesus in this week's readings (examples: lecturing, rebukes, parables). How did He vary teaching methods to fit His audiences? Give examples.

5. What could you generalize about the way God relates to people and/or human circumstances from any of this week's readings?

SCRIPTURES I WANT TO REMEMBER
AND ADDITIONAL NOTES

WEEK 4

Old Testament/New Testament

- o Day 1   Exodus 4-6/Matthew 14:22-36.
- o Day 2   Exodus 7-8/Matthew 15:1-20
- o Day 3   Exodus 9-11/Matthew
- o Day 4   Exodus 12-13/Matthew 16
- o Day 5   Exodus 14-15/Matthew 17
- o Day 6   Exodus 16-18/Matthew 18:1-20
- o Day 7   Exodus 19-20/Matthew 18:21-35

Focus scripture: Exodus 10:1-2/Matthew 17:20-21

QUESTIONS

1. When Moses first went to Pharaoh, the king increased the Israelites' work load, and they in turn blamed Moses. Look at Exodus 5:22-23. Have you felt this way recently? How did God respond to Moses? Do you think that this is the way that God usually responds to those who do His will but are not seeing good results?

2. List some ways that God showed His loving concern for His people in the chapters you read in the Old Testament this week. (One example might be the cloud and fiery pillar for guidance.) What are some equivalents today? (The Bible guides us like the cloud and fiery pillar did, for example.)

3. Compare the stories of the feeding of the four thousand with the feeding of the five thousand (Matthew 14:13-21). What details show that these were not two accounts of the same event?

4. Why do you think Jesus counseled Peter, James, and John not to tell about the Transfiguration until after His resurrection? When He talked about His coming death, did He tell the general public or just His disciples?

5. Was there a situation in your life this last week where you did as Jesus said in Matthew 18:15-17; or a time when you could have done this, but did not?

6. What could you generalize about the way God relates to people and/or human circumstances from any of this week's readings?

SCRIPTURES I WANT TO REMEMBER
AND ADDITIONAL NOTES

WEEK 5

Old Testament/New Testament

- o Day 1   Exodus 21-22/Matthew 19
- o Day 2   Exodus 23-24/Matthew 20:1-16
- o Day 3   Exodus 25-26/Matthew 20:17-34
- o Day 5   Exodus 29-30/Matthew 21:23-46
- o Day 6   Exodus 31-33/Matthew 22:1-22
- o Day 7   Exodus 34-35/Matthew 22:23-46

Focus scripture: Exodus 29:45-46/Matthew 21:21-22

QUESTIONS

1. We might be accustomed to looking at the precise instructions given to Moses for the tabernacle and its furnishings, and to use these as an example of how God is exacting in His expectations of how we worship Him. But what problems did God anticipate and thus eliminate by giving specific instructions? How is this true of all the time that God gives us rules that eliminate some choices for us? In what ways has life been simplified for you because you have submitted to some of God's rules?

2. We read that Bezalel was filled with the Spirit of God in order to enable him to be a great craftsman in decorating the tabernacle. This is a rare Old Testament mention of the work of the Holy Spirit. In what ways does the Spirit help us today in carrying out our life's professions?

3. When Jesus put His hands on the little children and prayed for them (Matthew 19:13), for what do you think He prayed?

4. Why do you think Jesus caused the fig tree to wither? How could this miracle be regarded as an "opposite" of His other miracles? What link did He say existed between faith and such miraculous works?

5. What could you generalize about the way God relates to people and/or human circumstances from any of this week's readings?

SCRIPTURES I WANT TO REMEMBER
AND ADDITIONAL NOTES

WEEK 6

Old Testament/New Testament

- o Day 1 Exodus 36-38/Matthew 23:1-22
- o Day 2 Exodus 39-40/Matthew 23:23-30
- o Day 3 Leviticus 1-3/Matthew 24:1-28
- o Day 4 Leviticus 4-5/Matthew 24:29-51
- o Day 5 Leviticus 6-7/Matthew 25:1-30
- o Day 6 Leviticus 8-10/Matthew 25:31-46
- o Day 7 Leviticus 11-12/Matthew 26:1-30

Focus scripture: Leviticus 5:17/Matthew 25:37-40

QUESTIONS

1. In Exodus 36, we see that the Lord had to actually restrain the grateful Israelites from giving more than was needed for the tabernacle and its furnishings. Is it possible today to give too much to the Lord of one's self and one's possessions? How do you as a couple determine when and what is "too much"?

2. In Leviticus 4, 5, and 6, the Lord distinguishes between intentional and unintentional sin. How do we know God held the Israelites responsible for both kinds of sin? In which type of sin was restitution required? Is there a "procedure" for Christians today by which we obtain forgiveness for intentional sin? For unintentional sin?

3. Who is the most difficult person you have to deal with? How can
    understanding Matthew 25:31-46 make it easier to deal with such
    difficult people?

4. What type of hymn do you suppose the disciples and Jesus sang
    before going to the Mount of Olives (Matthew 26:30)? What
    hymns that you sing would have been ones you would have
    suggested if you had been one of the apostles? Sing that hymn
    together now as you meditate on that night.

5. What could you generalize about the way God relates to people
    and/or human circumstances from any of this week's readings?

SCRIPTURES I WANT TO REMEMBER

AND ADDITIONAL NOTES

WEEK 7

Old Testament/New Testament

- o   Day 1   Leviticus 13/Matthew 26:31-50
- o   Day 2   Leviticus 14/Matthew 26:51-75
- o   Day 3   Leviticus 15-16/Matthew 27:1-26
- o   Day 4   Leviticus 17-18/Matthew 27:27-50
- o   Day 5   Leviticus 19-20/Matthew 27:51-66
- o   Day 6   Leviticus 21-22/Matthew 28:1-10
- o   Day 7   Leviticus 23-24/Matthew 28:11-20

Focus scripture: Leviticus 18:24-28/Matthew 28:5-7

QUESTIONS

1.   The Israelites placed their sins onto a goat, which was to be set free in the desert, carrying away their sins. How do you think that putting your faults once a year onto an animal could make you feel better? Who is our scapegoat today?

2.   Read over the unlawful sexual relations mentioned in Leviticus 18. What were the reasons for keeping oneself from such relations that God mentioned at the end of this chapter? How does God show the disgust that even the land has for such things?

3. When Jesus first prayed in the garden, Matthew says He asked, "May this cup be taken from me, yet not as I will, but as You will." Then later He prayed, "If it is not possible for this cup to be taken away unless I drink it, may Your will be done." What progression of thought do you see from the first prayer to the second one? How might that parallel the changes of attitude that we see in maturing Christians?

4. Why do you think that, when He was tried before the priests, Sanhedrin, and elders, Jesus answered their charges but refused to defend Himself against their charges when the same men accused Him before Pilate?

5. What could you generalize about the way God relates to people and/or human circumstances from any of this week's readings?

SCRIPTURES I WANT TO REMEMBER

AND ADDITIONAL NOTES

WEEK 8

Old Testament/New Testament

- o Day 1   Leviticus 25/Mark I
- o Day 2   Leviticus 26-27/Mark 2
- o Day 3   Numbers 1-2/Mark 3:1-19
- o Day 4   Numbers 3-4/Mark 3:20-35
- o Day 5   Numbers 5-6/Mark 4:1-20
- o Day 6   Numbers 7-8/Mark 4:21-41
- o Day 7   Numbers 9-11/Mark 5:1-20

Focus scripture: Leviticus 26:3-13/Mark 3:31-35

QUESTIONS

1. How did following the jubilee commandments in Leviticus 25 teach the Israelites to trust God to supply their needs? In what similar way will He today supply our needs?

2. What lesson do we learn from Leviticus 26:13 about the importance to God of human dignity? Just before, He'd said the Israelites were His servants. Does God want us to hold our heads high? What will be the result of tasting God's goodness and then rejecting His laws? (See Leviticus 26:14-25.)

3. Why do you think Jesus often told people He'd healed not to tell anyone? Did the people He healed obey? Why do you think this was so? What did He tell the demon-possessed man He healed in Mark 5?

4. In the parables of the growing seed and the mustard seed, what characteristic of the kingdom does Jesus emphasize? How do you think this concept affected His countrymen's understanding of their own roles as agents in the process?

5. What could you generalize about the way God relates to people and/or human circumstances from any of this week's readings?

SCRIPTURES I WANT TO REMEMBER
AND ADDITIONAL NOTES

WEEK 9

New Testament/Old Testament

- o   Day 1   Numbers 12-15/Mark 5:21-43
- o   Day 2   Numbers 16-19/Mark 6:1-56
- o   Day 3   Numbers 20-22/Mark 7:1-13
- o   Day 4   Numbers 23-25/Mark 7:14-37
- o   Day 5   Numbers 26-27/Mark 8:1-21
- o   Day 6   Numbers 28-30/Mark 8:22-38
- o   Day 7   Numbers 31-33/Mark 9:1-29

Focus scripture: Numbers 23:19-20/Mark 8:34-38

QUESTIONS

1. What promises had the Lord made to the Israelites that should have quieted their fears about the size and power of the Canaanites? What great problems are you facing today? What promises has God's Word made you about dealing with these problems?

2. In Numbers 15:37, God commanded the Israelites to sew tassels on their garments. What was the purpose of these tassels? When you are discouraged or tempted, what do you use as "tassels"?

3. When the disciples were given instructions to take nothing except a staff, who did Jesus assume would provide for them? Whom did the disciples have to trust in this arrangement?

4. What details of Mark's account would you point out to someone who believed that the feeding of the 5,000 was accomplished when all the members of the crowd shared lunches they had up until that point been unwilling to share? What details would you point out from the account of the feeding of the 4,000 to prove the same point?

5. What could you generalize about the way God relates to people and/or human circumstances from any of this week's readings?

SCRIPTURES I WANT TO REMEMBER
AND ADDITIONAL NOTES

WEEK 10

Old Testament/New Testament

- o Day 1   Numbers 34-36/Mark 9:30-50
- o Day 2   Deuteronomy 1-2/Mark 10:1-31
- o Day 3   Deuteronomy 3-4/Mark 10:32-52
- o Day 4   Deuteronomy 5-7/Mark 11:1-18
- o Day 5   Deuteronomy 8-10/Mark 11:19-33
- o Day 6   Deuteronomy 11-13/Mark 12:1-27
- o Day 7   Deuteronomy 14-16/Mark 12:28-44

Focus scripture: Deuteronomy 2:7/Mark 10:42-45

QUESTIONS

1. Deuteronomy is Moses' address to the people, reviewing for them the events of the past 40 years. How would you characterize the way Moses led the people? How did he encourage them when they were afraid of defeat? How did the people usually respond?

2. Deuteronomy 6:4-9 talks of teaching God's commandments in a day-to-day way. How do you encourage your mate to do this?

3. Read Mark 9:42-48. Can you identify anything in your life that is causing or tempting you to sin? How can you remove that influence from your life—or, if it is not possible to remove it, how can you aggressively deal with it?

4. In Mark chapter 11 we read of the cursing of the fig tree and the cleansing of the temple. What lessons do you think Jesus was teaching with His actions in these two incidents? How do these actions fit in with your overall concept of Jesus?

5. What could you generalize about the way God relates to people and/or human circumstances from any of this week's readings?

SCRIPTURES I WANT TO REMEMBER
AND ADDITIONAL NOTES

WEEK 11

Old Testament/ New Testament
- Day 1 Deuteronomy 17-19/Mark 13:1-20
- Day 2 Deuteronomy 20-22/Mark 13:21-37
- Day 3 Deuteronomy 23-25/Mark 14:1-26
- Day 4 Deuteronomy 26-27/Mark 14:27-53
- Day 5 Deuteronomy 28-29/Mark 14:54-72
- Day 6 Deuteronomy 30-31/Mark 15:1-25
- Day 7 Deuteronomy 32-34/Mark 15:26-47

Focus scripture: Deuteronomy 28:12/Mark 14:8-9

QUESTIONS

1. How has the Lord blessed your obedience to Him in times past? Look at Deuteronomy 28:1-14 and compare your blessings to those promised to the Israelites.

2. What happens to the person who hears God's commandments and thinks, "I will be safe, even though I persist in going my own way?" (See Deuteronomy 29:19.) What advice would you give such a person?

3. What characteristics of Peter do you see in the following incidents?

    a. His promise to never desert Jesus

    b. His cutting off the ear of the servant of the high priest

    c. His disowning Jesus

    d. His remorse after disowning Jesus

    Now look ahead to Mark chapter 16. Whom did the angel at the tomb tell the women to notify of the resurrection?

4. Why do you think Pilate was surprised to hear that Jesus had died so quickly? What does His "early" death tell you about the severity of the beatings He sustained before He was crucified?

5. What could you generalize about the way God relates to people and/or human circumstances from any of this week's readings?

SCRIPTURES I WANT TO REMEMBER
AND ADDITIONAL NOTES

WEEK 12

Old Testament/New Testament

- o   Day 1   Joshua 1-3/Mark 16
- o   Day 2   Joshua 4-6/Luke 1:1-20
- o   Day 3   Joshua 7-9/Luke 1:21-38
- o   Day 4   Joshua 10-12/Luke 1:39-56
- o   Day 5   Joshua 13-15/Luke 1:57-80
- o   Day 6   Joshua 16-18/Luke 2:1-24
- o   Day 7   Joshua 19-21/Luke 2:25-52

Focus scripture: Joshua 2:43-45/Luke 1:1-4

QUESTIONS

1.   What motivated Rahab to lie about the whereabouts of the spies? How do these same motivations move people today? How can a Christian capitalize on such motivations when we see them in the thoughts of nonbelievers?

2.   What was the mistake the men of Israel made when they were deciding whether or not to make a treaty with the Gibeonites? How can you encourage each other not to make this same mistake when you are faced with a decision?

3. What was Luke's purpose in writing his gospel? Was he an eyewitness of the events he described? Look at Luke 2:1-5 and list the details Luke included to verify his account. According to what Luke 1:1-4 says, what do you have in common with Luke, when you are teaching someone about Christ?

4. Contrast Mary's reaction to the angel's news, to the reaction of Zechariah. What logical questions did they each ask the angel?

5. What could you generalize about the way God relates to people and/or human circumstances from any of this week's readings?

SCRIPTURES I WANT TO REMEMBER

AND ADDITIONAL NOTES

WEEK 13

Old Testament/New Testament

- o   Day 1   Joshua 22-24/Luke 3
- o   Day 2   Judges 1-3/Luke 4:1-30
- o   Day 3   Judges 4-6/Luke 4:31-44
- o   Day 4   Judges 7-8/Luke 5:1-16
- o   Day 5   Judges 9-10/Luke 5:17-39
- o   Day 6   Judges 11-12/Luke 6:1-26
- o   Day 7   Judges 13-15/Luke 6:27-49

Focus scripture: Joshua 22:14/Luke 5:16; 6:12

QUESTIONS

1.   What was the misunderstanding in Joshua 22? Can you think of a time when you misunderstood someone's motives for doing something? What did Phineas do that could help you in a similar situation?

2.   What was the lesson God wanted Gideon to learn? How does God teach us that lesson today? When the Midianites suffered the great defeat in Judges 7, by whom were most of them killed? Who therefore could rightfully take credit for the victory?

3. In Luke 3:1-2, how does Luke again show his serious intent to
    establish his serious intent to establish his gospel as an historical
    document?

4. Compare the genealogy of Joseph with that of Mary in Matthew
    1. Where do they diverge?

5. What was the reaction of the people in the synagogue at Nazareth
    when Jesus told them He'd fulfilled the Isaiah prophecy? Why did
    their feelings toward him change so radically a short time later?

6. What could you generalize about the way God relates to people
    and/or human circumstances from any of this week's readings?

SCRIPTURES I WANT TO REMEMBER
AND ADDITIONAL NOTES

WEEK 14

Old Testament/New Testament

- o   Day 1   Judges 16-18/Luke 7:1-30
- o   Day 2   Judges 19-21/Luke 7:31-50
- o   Day 3   Ruth 1-4/Luke 8:1-25
- o   Day 4   1 Samuel 1-3/Luke 8:26-56
- o   Day 5   1 Samuel 4-6/Luke 9:1-17
- o   Day 6   1 Samuel 7-9/Luke 9:18-36
- o   Day 7   1 Samuel 10-12/Luke 9:37-62

Focus scripture: 1 Samuel 12:20-25/Luke 9:23-26

QUESTIONS

1. How could it be said of Micah and his mother (Judges 17-18) that they had good intentions? How did his having household idols and his own priest cause many others to sin and suffer? Does dedicating something to the Lord make that person or object exempt from sin and its effects?

2. In Ruth 2, what was it that attracted Boaz to Ruth? Are such qualities affected by aging? What ageless qualities attracted you to each other?

3. In Luke 7, who pleaded with Jesus to heal the son of the centurion? What did these people say was a good reason why Jesus should heal the son? What quality that Jesus possessed was the one with which the centurion could identify?

4. When the woman who'd been subject to bleeding for 12 years touched Jesus, He knew she had touched Him because He "felt power go out" from Him. What does this imply about the healing process? In your own experience, how is helping someone with an overpowering problem a draining experience? What are the compensations? What was Jesus' attitude toward the woman He'd healed?

5. What could you generalize about the way God relates to people and/or human circumstances from any of this week's readings?

SCRIPTURES I WANT TO REMEMBER
AND ADDITIONAL NOTES

WEEK 15

Old Testament / New Testament
- o   Day 1   1 Samuel 13-14/Luke 10:1-24
- o   Day 2   1 Samuel 15-16/Luke 10:25-42
- o   Day 3   1 Samuel 17-18/Luke 11:1-28
- o   Day 4   1 Samuel 19-21/Luke 11:29-54
- o   Day 5   1 Samuel 22-24/Luke 12:1-31
- o   Day 6   1 Samuel 25-26/Luke 12:32-59
- o   Day 7   1 Samuel 27-29/Luke 13:1-21

Focus scripture: 1 Samuel 17:34-37/Luke 11:9-13

QUESTIONS

1.   What pressures caused Saul to sin in 1 Samuel 13? Contrast that to how he sinned in 1 Samuel 15.

2.   How did Jonathan manifest his love for David? Did he ever seem to be jealous of David? What specific threat did David pose to Jonathan?

3. Is Luke 10:22-23 saying that God is arbitrary in the way He allows people to get to know Him? If your answer is yes, support it with scripture. If it is no, support it with scripture.

4. What are the six types of sin mentioned in Luke 11:37-54? Each of you examine your own lives carefully and identify any "Pharisaical" characteristics you find there.

5. What could you generalize about the way God relates to people and/or human circumstances from any of this week's readings?

SCRIPTURES I WANT TO REMEMBER
AND ADDITIONAL NOTES

WEEK 16

Old Testament / New Testament
- o Day 1 1 Samuel 30-31/Luke 13:22-35
- o Day 2 2 Samuel 1-2/Luke 14:1-14
- o Day 3 2 Samuel 3-5/Luke 14:25-35
- o Day 4 2 Samuel 6-8/Luke 15:1-10
- o Day 5 2 Samuel 9-11/Luke 15:11-32
- o Day 6 2 Samuel 12-13/ Luke 16
- o Day 7 2 Samuel 14-15/Luke 17:1-19

Focus scripture: 2 Samuel 7:22-24/Luke 17:5-6

QUESTIONS

1. When Michal, the wife of David, saw him leaping and rejoicing, what was the basis of her criticism? Do you think it was based on a valid point? What was David's defense of himself? Was it valid? Is it possible to wholeheartedly serve God without seeming foolish to some people?

2. How did David become popular with the people? Contrast this to the way Absalom gained his popularity. Which type of favor is easier to maintain over a long period of time?

3. In Luke 15 Jesus told parables about 3 things that were lost. Who rejoiced the most when they were found? Why in one parable was there bitterness on the part of others? Do you ever feel that way—or suspicious of motives—when someone is restored to Christian duty? How do you overcome such feelings?

4. Does Jesus' teachings about the servant in Luke 17:7-10 make it seem that the master was unreasonable? What do you think Jesus was saying about the nature of "duty?" Why are we considered unworthy when we only do our duty?

5. What could you generalize about the way God relates to people and/or human circumstances from any of this week's readings?

SCRIPTURES I WANT TO REMEMBER
AND ADDITIONAL NOTES

WEEK 17

Old Testament / New Testament

- o Day 1   2 Samuel 16-18/Luke 17:20-37
- o Day 2   2 Samuel 19-20/Luke 18:1-23
- o Day 3   2 Samuel 21-22/Luke 18:24-43
- o Day 4   2 Samuel 23-24/Luke 19:1-27
- o Day 5   1 Kings 1-2/Luke 19:28-48
- o Day 6   1 Kings 3-5/Luke 20:1-26
- o Day 7   1 Kings 6-7/Luke 20:27-47

Focus scripture: 2 Samuel 22:26-30/Luke 18:15-17

QUESTIONS

1. In this week's Old Testament readings, how was the history of God's people directly affected by good advice that was given to its leaders? How was it affected by bad advice? How would things have been better if Absalom had sought counsel from God instead of from men?

2. What were the conditions that God set for keeping someone of David's line on the throne? (1 Kings 2:1-4.) For Solomon's long life? (1 Kings 3:11-14.) For the promise that God would dwell among His people? (1 Kings 6:11-13.)

3. In Matthew 6:7 Jesus cautioned against praying with "many words." How does this fit in with his apparent encouragement of persistent prayer in Luke 18:1-8?

4. Look through this week's readings and observe the way Jesus handled questions that were posed by people who were trying to trap Him. Can you make any generalizations about how He dealt with such situations that might help you in a similar situation?

5. What could you generalize about the way God relates to people and/or human circumstances from any of this week's readings?

SCRIPTURES I WANT TO REMEMBER
AND ADDITIONAL NOTES

WEEK 18

Old Testament/New Testament

- o   Day 1   1 Kings 8-9/Luke 21:1-19
- o   Day 2   1 Kings 10-11/Luke 21:20-38
- o   Day 3   1 Kings 12-13/Luke 22:1-20
- o   Day 4   1 Kings 14-15/Luke 22:21-46
- o   Day 5   1 Kings 16-18/Luke 22:47-71
- o   Day 6   1 Kings 19-20/Luke 23:1-25
- o   Day 7   1 Kings 21-22/Luke 23:26-56

Focus scripture: 1 Kings 8:56-61/Luke 21:12-19

QUESTIONS

1. What does 1 Kings 11 say about the influence one's mate can have on your devotion to the Lord? What does this situation tell us about the effects of compromise in a marriage situation when religious matters are concerned?

2. Find instances in this week's Old Testament readings of how the Lord stated that He had raised up the rulers of Judah and of Israel. Is it true that even today God raises up both good and bad governmental leaders? What does this tell you about God's involvement in world affairs?

3. At the Last Supper, why was it logical that a discussion of who would betray Jesus led right into an argument about who among them was the greatest?

4. Find two examples from this week's readings where Jesus prayed for someone. What did He pray? What do you think was the effect on that person when He let it be known that He had so prayed?

5. What could you generalize about the way God relates to people and/or human circumstances from any of this week's readings?

SCRIPTURES I WANT TO REMEMBER
AND ADDITIONAL NOTES

WEEK 19

Old Testament/New Testament

- o   Day 1   2 Kings 1-3/Luke 24:1-35
- o   Day 2   2 Kings 4-6/Luke 24:36-53
- o   Day 3   2 Kings 7-9/John 1:1-28
- o   Day 4   2 Kings 10-12/John 1:29-51
- o   Day 5   2 Kings 13-14/John 2
- o   Day 6   2 Kings 15-16/John 3:1-18
- o   Day 7   2 Kings 17-18/John 3:19-36

Focus scripture: 2 Kings 17:7-22/John 3:5-8

QUESTIONS

1.   What was Gehazi's reasoning in asking for the gifts that Naaman had brought? Was he what you would call logical and reasonable in his thinking? Why was he condemned?

2.   When we look at Elisha in 2 Kings chapter 8, weeping as he pronounced the word of the Lord, we are filled with sympathy for the great man who could see into the future and yet know that he must let God control the destiny of Israel. How does being a servant of God today bring the same kind of burden on us?

3. The angel in Jesus' empty tomb reminded the women that Jesus had often predicted His own death and resurrection. Why do you think His followers hadn't really understood those predictions, nor apparently remembered them as the events were happening?

4. The gospels other than that of John seem concerned with documenting the events in the life of Jesus, beginning with the account of His birth. At what point in time does the account of John begin?

5. What could you generalize about the way God relates to people and/or human circumstances from any of this week's readings?

SCRIPTURES I WANT TO REMEMBER
AND ADDITIONAL NOTES

WEEK 20

Old Testament/ New Testament

- ○ Day 1   2 Kings 19-21/John 4:1-30
- ○ Day 2   2 Kings 22-23/John 4:31-54
- ○ Day 3   2 Kings 24-25/John 5:1-24
- ○ Day 4   1 Chronicles 1-3/John 5:25-47
- ○ Day 5   1 Chronicles 4-6/John 6:1-21
- ○ Day 6   1 Chronicles 7-9/John 6:22-44
- ○ Day 7   1 Chronicles 10-12/John 6:45-71

Focus scripture: 2 Kings 23:18-20/John 6:35-40

QUESTIONS

1. What reasons did God give for answering Hezekiah's prayer for a longer life? Does God really listen to our prayers today, and answer them by changing circumstances?

2. Much of this week's reading in the Old Testament is composed of genealogical records. Mostly they are just lists of names, as you have no doubt seen. Sometimes, though, there's a personal note, as in the case of Jabez in 1 Chronicles 4:9-10. If you were being listed in a chronology of your family as having died yesterday, what would you be remembered for? Is this what you want to be remembered for?

3. What do you suppose was Jesus' tone of voice when He asked the man at the pool of Bethesda (John 5), "Do you want to get well?" Why do you think He asked that question?

4. When the people in John 6 who had been miraculously fed by Jesus concluded that He was the Messiah, what did they want to do to Him? What does this tell you about their understanding of Jesus' power? About their conception of what the Messiah would do for them?

5. What could you generalize about the way God relates to people and/or human circumstances from any of this week's readings?

SCRIPTURES I WANT TO REMEMBER
AND ADDITIONAL NOTES

WEEK 21

Old Testament/ New Testament

- o   Day 1   1 Chronicles 13-15/John 7:1-27
- o   Day 2   1 Chronicles 16-18/John 7:28-53
- o   Day 3   1 Chronicles 19-21/John 8:1-27
- o   Day 4   1 Chronicles 22-24/John 8:28-59
- o   Day 5   1 Chronicles 25-27/John 9:1-23
- o   Day 6   1 Chronicles 28-29/John 9:24-41
- o   Day 7   2 Chronicles 1-3/John 10:1-21

Focus scripture: 1 Chronicles 16:8-13/John 8:31-32

QUESTIONS

1. In 1 Chronicles 17 we see David wanting to build a house for the Lord. What motivated this desire? What did God say about David's intention? How did David respond when God told him that his son, not he, would be the one to build the temple? How do you think you would have reacted had you been in David's place?

2. What did David say in 1 Chronicles 29 about attitudes in giving? Are your attitudes like those of David? What relationship do you see between David's giving and his desire that others do so too? What is the relationship in your life between your giving and your wholehearted devotion to God?

3. The Pharisees were condemned by Christ because they made false assumptions. They assumed, for example, that keeping the Sabbath was of such great importance that no work—even beneficial service to others—could be performed. They also assumed that Jesus was a Galilean and therefore could not be the Messiah, who was prophesied to come from Bethlehem. What false assumptions have you, in the past, made about what God expects of you? How can John 7:24 help you avoid making false assumptions?

4. What do you suppose Jesus wrote on the ground (John 8:6-8)?

5. What could you generalize about the way God relates to people and/or human circumstances from any of this week's readings?

SCRIPTURES I WANT TO REMEMBER
AND ADDITIONAL NOTES

WEEK 22

Old Testament/ New Testament

- o   Day 1   2 Chronicles 4-6/John 10:22-42
- o   Day 2   2 Chronicles 7-9/John 11:1-29
- o   Day 3   2 Chronicles 10-12/John 11:30-57
- o   Day 4   2 Chronicles 13-14/John 12:1-26
- o   Day 5   2 Chronicles 15-16/John 12:27-50
- o   Day 6   2 Chronicles 17-18/John 13:1-20
- o   Day 7   2 Chronicles 19-20/John 13:21-38

Focus scripture: 2 Chronicles 15:12-15/John 12:23-36

QUESTIONS

1.   What requests did Solomon ask of God when he dedicated the temple? What promises did God make to Solomon (2 Chronicles 7)? How are these promises true in principle for us today?

2.   Look at the life of Asa (2 Chronicles 15-16). Whose advice did he seek in his life? Who gave him good counsel from God? How was he treated? Who else gave him counsel? What were the results?

3. Look at John chapter 9 and find where Jesus said why it was that the man was born blind. Now look at chapter 11. What did Jesus say was the purpose behind the sickness of Lazarus? In both these cases, where Jesus "used" someone's apparent misfortune to teach a lesson, who benefited most from the events that transpired? Can you make a generalization from that about "bad" things that have happened in your life?

4. Why do you suppose Jesus wept at the tomb of Lazarus?

5. What could you generalize about the way God relates to people and/or human circumstances from any of this week's readings?

SCRIPTURES I WANT TO REMEMBER
AND ADDITIONAL NOTES

WEEK 23

Old Testament/ New Testament

- o Day 1   2 Chronicles 21-22/John 14
- o Day 3   2 Chronicles 25-27/John 16
- o Day 4   2 Chronicles 28-29/John 17
- o Day 5   2 Chronicles 30-31/John 18:1-8
- o Day 6   2 Chronicles 32-33/John 18:19-40
- o Day 7   2 Chronicles 34-36/John 19:1-16

Focus scripture: 2 Chronicles 36:15-17/John 14:12-14

QUESTIONS

1. Contrast the death and burial of Jehoram (2 Chronicles 21) to the death and burial of Jehoida (2 Chronicles 24). What happened to the people's morality and the political scene after the death of each?

2. Contrast the message that Sennacherib king of Assyria sent to Hezekiah, to the message that Neco king of Egypt sent to Josiah in the following points:

    a. Which foreign king claimed to have a message from God?

b. Which foreign king respected God?

c. Did either of the foreign kings say that there was a way to avoid the coming destruction? For what do we remember Hezekiah and Josiah?

3. List the reasons Jesus gave in John chapters 14 and 15 for why we should not be troubled or afraid.

4. Show from this week's New Testament readings examples of how Jesus and the Holy Spirit are in subjection to the Father.

5. What could you generalize about the way God relates to people and/or human circumstances from any of this week's readings?

SCRIPTURES I WANT TO REMEMBER

AND ADDITIONAL NOTES

WEEK 24

Old Testament/ New Testament

- o Day 1 Ezra 1-2/John 19:17-42
- o Day 2 Ezra 3-5/John 20
- o Day 3 Ezra 6-8/John 21
- o Day 4 Ezra 9-10/Acts 1
- o Day 5 Nehemiah 1-3/Acts 2:1-21
- o Day 6 Nehemiah 4-6/Acts 2:22-47
- o Day 7 Nehemiah 7-9/Acts 3

Focus scripture: Ezra 8:21-23/Acts 2:42-47

QUESTIONS

1. The men of Trans-Euphrates tried to appeal to Artaxerxes by saying that the rebuilding of Jerusalem would hurt Artaxerxes' revenue from that area. Later, when Darius decreed that the temple's restoration was not to be hindered, from where did he decree that the revenues for this project should come (Ezra 6:8)? (Does this instance or any other in the Bible indicate to you that God might have a sense of humor?)

2. In Nehemiah chapter 4, what five people (or groups of people) criticized the wall-builders? What did Nehemiah say? What did he do? Who or what did Nehemiah say frustrated the plots of the critical people (Nehemiah 4:15)?

3. How did Jesus literally "serve" the disciples on the shores of the lake in John 21?

4. Do you think Peter made his listeners feel guilty on the day of Pentecost, and later in his sermon at Solomon's Porch? Was that good or bad? Is making someone feel guilty for sinning an effective way to bring them to repentance? Why or why not?

5. What could you generalize about the way God relates to people and/or human circumstances from any of this week's readings?

SCRIPTURES I WANT TO REMEMBER
AND ADDITIONAL NOTES

WEEK 25

Old Testament/ New Testament

- o Day 1   Nehemiah 10-11/Acts 4:1-22
- o Day 2   Nehemiah 12-13/Acts 4:23-47
- o Day 3   Esther 1-2/Acts 5:1-21
- o Day 4   Esther 3-5/Acts 5:22-42
- o Day 5   Esther 6-8/Acts 6
- o Day 6   Esther 9-10/Acts 7:1-21
- o Day 7   Job 1-2/Acts 7:22-60

Focus scripture: Esther 4:12-14/Acts 4:32-35

QUESTIONS

1. What were Nehemiah's actions when he returned to Jerusalem? Did any of them seem extreme? Did Nehemiah seem proud or ashamed of his reforms? From what you know of secular history and the New Testament, were the Jews faithful to God from this point on or did they slip in and out of idolatry as they had before?

2. Read what Mordecai told Esther in Esther 4:12-14. What does this tell you about the way in which God achieves His purposes? What role do individuals have in carrying out His plans? Do these verses indicate that God puts people in positions of leadership in order to

further His plans? What was Esther's attitude in carrying out Mordecai's instructions to go to the king?

3. Do you think Gamaliel's advice in Acts 5 to the Sanhedrin—that they shouldn't oppose the apostles—was based on sound reasoning? What did Gamaliel assume about the amount of power that the apostles had in and of themselves? Was Gamaliel's conclusion one that would hold true today? Why or why not?

4. What characteristics of the Jews did Stephen illustrate when he gave the outline of Jewish history in his last sermon?

5. What could you generalize about the way God relates to people and/or human circumstances from any of this week's readings?

SCRIPTURES I WANT TO REMEMBER
AND ADDITIONAL NOTES

WEEK 26

Old Testament/ New Testament

- o Day 1   Job 3-4/Acts 8:1-25
- o Day 2   Job 5-7/Acts 8:26-40
- o Day 3   Job 8-10/Acts 9:1-21
- o Day 4   Job 11-13/Acts 9:22-43
- o Day 5   Job 14-16/Acts 10:1-23
- o Day 6   Job 17-19/Acts 10:24-48
- o Day 7   Job 20-21/Acts 11:1-18

Focus scripture: Job 13:15/Acts 8:36-37

QUESTIONS

1. From what Job—a righteous man—said about suffering in chapter 3, can we expect to be at peace when we are undergoing great trials? Did Job assign blame for his troubles to anyone or anything?

2. How does Job, in chapter 16, show that he understands his situation, both from his friends' point of view as well as from his own? What would he do differently if their roles were reversed? What can you conclude from this that would help you when you are counseling with someone who is suffering?

3. Do you think the Christians of the first century would say that "persecution" was all bad? (Were there ever any good results from it?)

4. What did the Lord say to Ananias that He wanted to show Saul?

5. Why do you think the widows of Joppa brought clothes Dorcas had made and showed them to Peter? What effect do you think this had on Peter?

6. What could you generalize about the way God relates to people and/or human circumstances from any of this week's readings?

SCRIPTURES I WANT TO REMEMBER

AND ADDITIONAL NOTES

WEEK 27

Old Testament/ New Testament

- o   Day 1   Job 22-24/Acts 11:19-30
- o   Day 2   Job 25-27/Acts 12
- o   Day 3   Job 28-29/Acts 13:1-25
- o   Day 4   Job 30-31/Acts 13:26-52
- o   Day 5   Job 32-33/Acts 14
- o   Day 6   Job 34-35/Acts 15:1-21
- o   Day 7   Job 36-37/Acts 15:22-41

Focus scripture: Job 27:11/Acts 14:15-17

QUESTIONS

1. Eliphaz, Bildad, and Zophar unjustly accused Job of both hidden and open sin. In reviewing what these men said overall, not including their accusations against Job, would you say that they spoke truth? Was this helpful to Job? Why or why not?

2. Job's frustration seems to be mainly due to the fact that he couldn't present his side of the story—plead his own case—to God. How would you advise someone who felt as Job did?

3. We learn in Acts 11:25 that Barnabus went to Tarsus to look for Saul. How is his partnership with Saul a reflection of the church's new spirit of love and acceptance? What does it tell you about Barnabus personally?

4. How is the reaction of Rhoda in Acts 12 characteristic of how we Christians are when we receive answer to prayer? How was the reaction of the other Christians in verses 15-16 characteristic of another way we view answered prayer? List some things for which you have been praying earnestly. How do you plan to react when God answers these prayers?

5. What could you generalize about the way God relates to people and/or human circumstances from any of this week's readings?

SCRIPTURES I WANT TO REMEMBER
AND ADDITIONAL NOTES

WEEK 28

Old Testament New Testament

- o Day 1   Job 38-40/Acts 16:1-21
- o Day 2   Job 41-42/Acts 16:22-40
- o Day 3   Psalms 1-3/Acts 17:1-15
- o Day 4   Psalms 4-6/Acts 17:16-34
- o Day 5   Psalms 7-9/Acts 18
- o Day 6   Psalms 10-12/Acts 19:1-20
- o Day 7   Psalms 13-15/Acts 19:21-41

Focus scripture: Psalm 1:1-6/Acts 17:11-12

QUESTIONS

1. When God finally spoke to Job, it was in questions, not answers. What were some of the questions He asked him? Why did God ask Job these questions? What, in chapter 42, did Job conclude?

2. Find statements in the first 15 psalms that show that David understood that God prospers those who love Him and punishes the wicked. How do you think David's understanding of this principle differed from Job's friends' understanding? Find statements in the first 15 psalms that show that David understood,

too, that the wicked sometimes seem to prosper at the expense of the weak.

3. What was Paul's purpose in Acts 16:37 in insisting that he and Silas be escorted from the jail? What effect do you think this had in future times whenever there was a confrontation between Christians and Roman authorities?

4. How did Priscilla and Aquila deal with the "holes" in Apollos' theology? Are there people you know who have similar gaps in their religious thinking? What did Priscilla and Aquila do that you could do with these people you know? Can you as a couple name such an individual and right now schedule a time to follow the example of Priscilla and Aquila?

5. What could you generalize about the way God relates to people and/or human circumstances from any of this week's readings?

SCRIPTURES I WANT TO REMEMBER
AND ADDITIONAL NOTES

WEEK 29

Old Testament/ New Testament

- o Day 1   Psalms 16-17/Acts 20:1-16
- o Day 2   Psalms 18-19/Acts 20:17-38
- o Day 3   Psalms 20-22/Acts 21:1-17
- o Day 4   Psalms 23-25/Acts 21:18-40
- o Day 5   Psalms 26-28/Acts 22
- o Day 6   Psalms 29-30/Acts 23:1-15
- o Day 7   Psalms 31-32/Acts 23:16-35

Focus scripture: Psalm 20:4-5/Acts 20:35

QUESTIONS

1. Read Psalm 26. Could you make the statements David made in this psalm? Why or why not? What changes would be necessary in your life in order for you to be able to speak as David spoke?

2. What qualities of God are described in Psalm 29? Praise Him now, in prayer, for these qualities.

3. Look at the context of Acts 20:35. When Paul quoted Jesus as saying, "It is more blessed to give than to receive," what was Paul talking about giving and receiving?

4. Compare Paul's sermon in Acts 23 to some sermons he'd preached previously. Show from each examples of how Paul was adept at tailoring a sermon to a particular audience's beliefs about God and religion in general, and appealing to those beliefs which were true.

5. What could you generalize about the way God relates to people and/or human circumstances from any of this week's readings?

SCRIPTURES I WANT TO REMEMBER
AND ADDITIONAL NOTES

WEEK 30

Old Testament/ New Testament

- o Day 1   Psalm 33-34/Acts 24
- o Day 2   Psalm 35-36/Acts 25
- o Day 3   Psalm 37-39/Acts 26
- o Day 4   Psalm 40-42/Acts 27:1-26
- o Day 5   Psalm 43-45/Acts 27:27-44
- o Day 6   Psalm 46-48/Acts 28
- o Day 7   Psalms 49-50/Romans 1

Focus scripture: Psalm 37:3-4/Romans 1:16-17

QUESTIONS

1. How could David say with authority the things he said in Psalm 34?

2. Does Psalm 37 promise "smooth sailing" for those who trust in God? If not, what does it promise?

3. For what "needs" do you think Paul's friends provided (Acts 24:23; 27:3)?

4. What do you see from Paul's behavior in Acts 27 that would help you be a good leader in a time of crisis?

5. How does the closing of the book of Acts seem to be an appropriate introduction for the book of Romans?

6. What could you generalize about the way God relates to people and/or human circumstances from any of this week's readings?

SCRIPTURES I WANT TO REMEMBER
AND ADDITIONAL NOTES

WEEK 31

Old Testament/New Testament

- o   Day 1 Psalms 51-53/Romans 2
- o   Day 2 Psalms 54-56/Romans 3
- o   Day 3 Psalms 57-59/Romans 4
- o   Day 4 Psalms 60-62/Romans 5
- o   Day 5 Psalms 63-65/Romans 6
- o   Day 6 Psalms 66-67/Romans 7
- o   Day 7 Psalms 68-69/Romans 8:1-17

Focus scripture: Psalm 51:10-12/Romans 3:23-24

QUESTIONS

1. Many of this week's psalms are imprecatory psalms: that is, they are asking for vengeance on enemies. Find an example of this from this week's readings. How do you reconcile such writings with the fact that God said that David was a man after His own heart?

2. Psalm 66:16-20 tells of how David received love from God. Have you ever had a sin in your life that you "cherished" (verse 18)? How complete was your repentance while you felt that way? How did your life change after you stopped cherishing that sin?

3. How does Paul say that lawless people pervert the truth about how God really is (Romans 1:21-24)? How did Jews cause His name to be blasphemed (2:17-21)?

4. When Paul spoke of the law, did he regard it as a good thing or bad? Support your answers from Scripture.

5. What could you generalize about the way God relates to people and/or human circumstances from any of this week's readings?

SCRIPTURES I WANT TO REMEMBER

AND ADDITIONAL NOTES

WEEK 32

Old Testament/ New Testament

- o   Day 1   Psalms 70-71/Romans 8:18-39
- o   Day 2   Psalms 72-73/Romans 9:1-15
- o   Day 3   Psalms 74-76/Romans 9:16-33
- o   Day 4   Psalms 77-78/Romans 10
- o   Day 5   Psalms 79-80/Romans 11:1-18
- o   Day 6   Psalms 81-83/Romans 11:19-30
- o   Day 7   Psalms 84-86/Romans 12

Focus scripture: Psalm 84:10-11/Romans 8:26-27

QUESTIONS

1. What conclusions did Asaph draw in Psalm 73 about the question that so plagued Job: "Is it just for the wicked to prosper on earth?"

2. In Psalm 77, how did Asaph say we can reassure ourselves that God's love is unfailing? How did Asaph continue that thought into Psalm 78? When you are discouraged, do you do this?

3. List all the "bad" things you can think of that happened to you during this last week. How can Romans 8:28 help you in dealing with problems like these?

4. What reason did Paul give in Romans 11 for his diligence in preaching to the Gentiles as well as to his own people the Jews?

5. How could it be said that Paul "shifted gears" when he got to chapter 12?

6. What could you generalize about the way God relates to people and/or human circumstances from any of this week's readings?

SCRIPTURES I WANT TO REMEMBER
AND ADDITIONAL NOTES

WEEK 33

Old Testament/ New Testament

- o   Day 1   Psalm 87-88/Romans 13
- o   Day 2   Psalm 89-90/Romans 14
- o   Day 3   Psalm 91-93/Romans 15:1-13
- o   Day 4   Psalm 94-96/Romans 15:14-33
- o   Day 5   Psalm 97-99/Romans 16
- o   Day 6   Psalm 100-102/1 Corinthians 1
- o   Day 7   Psalm 103-103/1 Corinthians 2

Focus scripture: Psalm 93:1-5/Romans 13:9-10

QUESTIONS

1. Psalm 88 is certainly one of the most depressing passages in all scripture. How would you describe this man's life as it is portrayed in this psalm? Why would God allow a psalm like this in with the more uplifting psalms in this book?

2. From what dangers does this psalm say that God will protect the believer? In what specific ways does God promise to help? In which of these ways have you been helped this week?

3. Read Romans 13:1-7 and then comment on whether or not you think it is pleasing to God for missionaries in foreign countries to teach converts to disobey civil authorities. Are there ever circumstances where civil disobedience is justified in God's sight?

4. Paul spoke extensively of the law in the first chapters of Romans. What does he say in chapter 13 is the summation of the law? Who else said that before Paul?

5. What could you generalize about the way God relates to people and/or human circumstances from any of this week's readings?

SCRIPTURES I WANT TO REMEMBER
AND ADDITIONAL NOTES

WEEK 34

Old Testament/ New Testament

- o Day 1   Psalms 105-106/1 Corinthians 3
- o Day 2   Psalms 107-109/1 Corinthians 4
- o Day 3   Psalms 110-112/1 Corinthians 5
- o Day 4   Psalms 113-115/1 Corinthians 6
- o Day 5   Psalms 116-118/1 Corinthians 7:1-19
- o Day 6   Psalm 119:1-88/1 Corinthians 7:20-40
- o Day 7   Psalm 119:89-176/1 Corinthians 8

Focus scripture: Psalm 119:9-11/1 Corinthians 3:10-15

QUESTIONS

1. Psalms 105 and 106 are like a mini-history course in God's dealings with the Israelites. Skim over both these psalms. What, apparently, were the events that had the most meaning to this psalmist? Why do you think that is so?

2. Psalm 110 is a psalm that prophesies Christ. Find details of this psalm that apply to Jesus. How do you think the people of David viewed this psalm?

3. What do you think 1 Corinthians 3:15 means?

4. How is 1 Corinthians 7:2-5 a part of your marriage? How can you make it more a part of your marriage?

5. What could you generalize about the way God relates to people and/or human circumstances from any of this week's readings?

SCRIPTURES I WANT TO REMEMBER
AND ADDITIONAL NOTES

WEEK 35

Old Testament/ New Testament

- o Day 1   Psalms 120-122 1 Corinthians 9
- o Day 2   Psalms 123-125/1 Corinthians 10:1-18
- o Day 3   Psalms 126-128/1 Corinthians 10:19-33
- o Day 4   Psalms 129-131/1 Corinthians 11:1-16
- o Day 5   Psalms 132-134/1 Corinthians 11:17-34
- o Day 6   Psalms 135-136/1 Corinthians 12
- o Day 7   Psalms 137-139/1 Corinthians 13

Focus scripture: Psalm 131/1 Corinthians 10:12-13

QUESTIONS

1. For whom did David want peace in Psalm 122? Whom would this peace ultimately glorify? What had Jerusalem come to signify in the minds of God's people? (Look at Psalm 137 for confirmation of this.)

2. How did David feel about the fact that God knew him so intimately? How does it make you feel to know that God knows you that well, too?

3. Which four "rights" did Paul say he had, but which he had not demanded for himself? Which of these rights do you have? What would be your reaction if you suddenly learned you were no longer entitled to these things?

4. Is 1 Corinthians 12:27 an acknowledgement that different religious denominations are inevitable? Why or why not?

5. What could you generalize about the way God relates to people and/or human circumstances from any of this week's readings?

SCRIPTURES I WANT TO REMEMBER

AND ADDITIONAL NOTES

WEEK 36

Old Testament/ New Testament

- o   Day 1   Psalms 140-142/1 Corinthians 14:1-20
- o   Day 2   Psalms 143-145/1 Corinthians 14:21-40
- o   Day 3   Psalms 146-147/1 Corinthians 15:1-28
- o   Day 4   Psalms 148-150/1 Corinthians 15:29-58
- o   Day 5   Proverbs 1-2/1 Corinthians 16
- o   Day 6   Proverbs 3-5/2 Corinthians I
- o   Day 7   Proverbs 6-7/2 Corinthians 2

Focus scripture: Proverbs 3:5-6/2 Corinthians 1:3-5

QUESTIONS

1. Look over this week's readings in Psalms. Name at least three specific ways in which David asked God to help him in his daily fight against evil. How does God help you today in the same ways?

2. Why did Solomon say in Proverbs 1:1-7 that he had written down the proverbs?

3. What points from 1 Corinthians 15 would you show to someone who claims to be a Christian but does not believe in the literal resurrection of the body?

4. How can 2 Corinthians 1:3-11 help you deal with problems you have faced this past week?

5. What could you generalize about the way God relates to people and/or human circumstances from any of this week's readings?

SCRIPTURES I WANT TO REMEMBER

AND ADDITIONAL NOTES

WEEK 37

Old Testament/ New Testament

- o Day 1 Proverbs 8-9/2 Corinthians 3
- o Day 2 Proverbs 10-12/2 Corinthians 4
- o Day 3 Proverbs 13-15/2 Corinthians 5
- o Day 4 Proverbs 16-18/2 Corinthians 6
- o Day 5 Proverbs 19-21/2 Corinthians 7
- o Day 6 Proverbs 22-24/2 Corinthians 8
- o Day 7 Proverbs 25-26/2 Corinthians 9

Focus scripture: Proverbs 16:24/2 Corinthians 4:16-18

QUESTIONS

1. Of what importance to Solomon was wisdom? How do you think he would have defined wisdom? How did he obtain his wisdom? How does the personification of Wisdom found in Proverbs 9 contrast with the personification of Folly found there?

2. The Proverbs speak much about the influence of the tongue. Find examples from this week's readings where the following are discussed:

   a. the words of an adulteress

    b. the influence of flattery

    c. lying

    d. encouragement

    e. gossip

3. If someone described each of you in a letter, like Paul did the Corinthian believers, what would you like to have that letter say? How would you like your marriage described?

4. List some of the benefits mentioned in 2 Corinthians 9 that generous giving will bring to you.

5. What could you generalize about the way God relates to people and/or human circumstances from any of this week's readings?

SCRIPTURES I WANT TO REMEMBER
AND ADDITIONAL NOTES

WEEK 38

Old Testament/ New Testament

- ○ Day 1 Proverbs 27-29/2 Corinthians 10
- ○ Day 2 Proverbs 30-31/2 Corinthians 11:1-15
- ○ Day 3 Ecclesiastes 1-3/2 Corinthians 11:16-33
- ○ Day 4 Ecclesiastes 4-6/2 Corinthians 12
- ○ Day 5 Ecclesiastes 7-9/2 Corinthians 13
- ○ Day 6 Ecclesiastes 10-12/Galatians I
- ○ Day 7 Song of Solomon 1-3/Galatians 2

Focus scripture: Proverbs 31:10-31/2 Corinthians 10:17-18

QUESTIONS

1. "Meaningless" or "vanity" is a recurrent theme in Ecclesiastes. But in 3:11-15 and 5:18-20 Solomon speaks confidently of things that are not meaningless or vain. How do you reconcile this with the rest of Ecclesiastes? What did Solomon conclude at the end of Ecclesiastes?

2. What do the two lovers in Song of Solomon say and do that you could say and do to improve your marriage?

3. What would you identify in your life as your "thorn in the flesh?" How can God's power become perfect, as Paul said, through weakness?

4. What types of internal problems does Galatians 1 and 2 show us existed in the early church? How did the leadership handle disagreements on doctrine? What can you conclude from this that would help you when you see disagreements between sincere believers?

5. What could you generalize about the way God relates to people and/or human circumstances from any of this week's readings?

SCRIPTURES I WANT TO REMEMBER
AND ADDITIONAL NOTES

WEEK 39

Old Testament/ New Testament

- o   Day 1   Song of Solomon 4-5/Galatians 3
- o   Day 2   Song of Solomon 6-8/Galatians 4
- o   Day 3   Isaiah 1-2/Galatians 5
- o   Day 4   Isaiah 3-4/Galatians 6
- o   Day 5   Isaiah 5-6/Ephesians 1
- o   Day 6   Isaiah 7-8/Ephesians 2
- o   Day 7   Isaiah 9-10/Ephesians 3

Focus scripture: Song of Solomon 8:6-7/Galatians 3:26-29

QUESTIONS

1. In Isaiah 1:18-20, God gives a condition on which He will forgive all past sins. What is this condition? How is it a "reasonable" condition? What would be the result in society if God forgave sin without people keeping this condition?

2. Try to imagine seeing God as Isaiah recorded in chapter 6. Which of His qualities are emphasized? How does this make you feel about your relationship to God?

3. Is there a contradiction between Galatians 6:2 and 6:5? Explain.

4. Ephesians chapters 1 and 2 speak over and over of how God planned things for us before the world's creation. Go verse by verse and list what God's purpose and foreknowledge wanted for us.

5. What could you generalize about the way God relates to people and/or human circumstances from any of this week's readings?

SCRIPTURES I WANT TO REMEMBER
AND ADDITIONAL NOTES

Just You, Me and God   169

WEEK 40

Old Testament/ New Testament

- o Day 1   Isaiah 11-13/Ephesians 4
- o Day 2   Isaiah 14-16/Ephesians 5:1-16
- o Day 3   Isaiah 17-19/Ephesians 5:17-33
- o Day 4   Isaiah 20-22/Ephesians 6
- o Day 5   Isaiah 23-25/Philippians 1
- o Day 6   Isaiah 26-27/Philippians 2
- o Day 7   Isaiah 28-29/Philippians 3

Focus scripture: Isaiah 12:4-6/Philippians 3:7-11

QUESTIONS

1. How do you think the Jewish people reacted when Isaiah pronounced his prophecy about Egypt in chapter 21? Why? What part did Egypt play in the early life of Jesus?

2. In 28:23-29, Isaiah is saying that God deals with different people in different ways, and He may discipline one person in one manner in one instance, and another way in a different circumstance. How does this show His wisdom? Can you think of examples that would illustrate this from your own life? What relationship does this concept have to 29:14-16?

3. Why does Ephesians 5:21 say we should submit to one another? In what ways does a wife submit to her husband that mirrors how the church submits to Christ? In what ways does a husband love his wife such that it mirrors how Christ loves the church?

4. Make a list of accomplishments of your lives like Paul did in Philippians 3:4-6. List things like your upbringing, education, Bible knowledge, etc. Now spend time memorizing Philippians 3:7-11.

5. What could you generalize about the way God relates to people and/or human circumstances from any of this week's readings?

SCRIPTURES I WANT TO REMEMBER
AND ADDITIONAL NOTES

WEEK 41

Old Testament/ New Testament

- o Day 1 Isaiah 30-31/Philippians 4
- o Day 2 Isaiah 32-33/Colossians 1
- o Day 3 Isaiah 34-36/Colossians 2
- o Day 4 Isaiah 37-38/Colossians 3
- o Day 5 Isaiah 39-40/Colossians 4
- o Day 6 Isaiah 41-42/1 Thessalonians 1
- o Day 7 Isaiah 43-44/1 Thessalonians 2

Focus scripture: Isaiah 35:3-4/Philippians 4:4-7

QUESTIONS

1. What do you think was God's purpose in warning in Isaiah chapter 34 about the judgements that would come against them? Are these warnings in the Bible for today's people, too? If so, explain. If not, why are they there?

2. Was the situation hopeless, from a human point of view, when Sennacherib's messengers told Hezekiah's men that Jerusalem would be destroyed? What action did Hezekiah take? What did God say in 37:21 was the cause of His actions against the Assyrian king?

3. What specific promises are made in Philippians 4 about God's supplying us with things we need? What things are you in need of right now? Can God supply these things? What did Paul say about his own attitudes toward needs? To what extent do you feel the same way?

4. In Colossians 2:16-23 Paul lists several practices in which people engage which, instead of bringing us closer to God, actually cut us off from Him. What are such practices? What alternatives does Paul give in chapter 3?

5. What could you generalize about the way God relates to people and/or human circumstances from any of this week's readings?

SCRIPTURES I WANT TO REMEMBER
AND ADDITIONAL NOTES

WEEK 42

Old Testament New Testament

- o   Day 1   Isaiah 45-46/1 Thessalonians 3
- o   Day 2   Isaiah 47-49/1 Thessalonians 4
- o   Day 3   Isaiah 50-52/1 Thessalonians 5:1-13
- o   Day 4   Isaiah 53-55/1 Thessalonians 5:14-28
- o   Day 5   Isaiah 56-58/2 Thessalonians 1
- o   Day 6   Isaiah 59-61/2 Thessalonians 2
- o   Day 7   Isaiah 62-64/2 Thessalonians 3

Focus scripture: Isaiah 55:1-11/1 Thessalonians 5:16-18

QUESTIONS

1. Isaiah spoke of Cyrus 100 years before he ruled. What does this tell you about God's involvement in the lives of non-believing rulers? Look at 45:3-6. Does God's leadership of such men require their knowledge or consent? What is God's ultimate aim in exalting such rulers?

2. Which descriptions of the great Servant in Isaiah 52-54 show this to be a description of Jesus?

3. Does 1 Thessalonians 4:11-12 advocate that Christians keep themselves separate from unbelievers? What kind of dependence is spoken of in verse 12? In what way can we and should we be dependent upon nonbelievers?

4. This week's New Testament readings showed how Paul dealt with special fears that the Thessalonians had concerning persecution and "the day of the Lord." Look back through both Thessalonians letters and list what God has promised to:

   a. Christians

   b. non-believers when that day arrives

5. What could you generalize about the way that God relates to people and/or human circumstances from any of this week's readings?

SCRIPTURES I WANT TO REMEMBER
AND ADDITIONAL NOTES

WEEK 43

Old Testament/ New Testament

- o   Day 1   Isaiah 65-66/1 Timothy 1-2
- o   Day 2   Jeremiah 1-2/1 Timothy 3
- o   Day 3   Jeremiah 3-5/1 Timothy 4
- o   Day 4   Jeremiah 6-8/1 Timothy 5
- o   Day 5   Jeremiah 9-11/1 Timothy 6
- o   Day 6   Jeremiah 12-14/2 Timothy 1
- o   Day 7   Jeremiah 15-17/2 Timothy 2

Focus scripture: Jeremiah 9:23-24/1 Timothy 4:13-16

QUESTIONS

1. What does Jeremiah 7:1-15 say about the dangers of relying on the fact that you are a member of the "right church"? What indications do you see in verses 21-24 of what might be called cafeteria religion (picking and choosing what you will and will not obey)?

2. Have you ever wept, like Jeremiah, for those against whom God's wrath will come? How is the fate of Judah like the fate of your lost neighbors and friends?

3. Pray together now, with "requests, intercessions, and thanksgiving" for your national, state, and local government leaders, so that you can "live peaceful and quiet lives in all godliness and holiness."

4. List the different types of people talked about in 1 Timothy 5, such as old women, young men, widows, etc. Then put the name of someone you know who fits that description. Reading what Paul said about such people, evaluate what your role should be toward these individuals.

5. What could you generalize about the way God relates to people and/or human circumstances from any of this week's readings?

SCRIPTURES I WANT TO REMEMBER
AND ADDITIONAL NOTES

WEEK 44

Old Testament/ New Testament

- o   Day 1   Jeremiah 18-19/2 Timothy 3
- o   Day 2   Jeremiah 20-21/2 Timothy 4
- o   Day 3   Jeremiah 22-23/Titus 1
- o   Day 4   Jeremiah 24-26/Titus 2
- o   Day 5   Jeremiah 27-29/Titus 3
- o   Day 6   Jeremiah 30-31/Philemon
- o   Day 7   Jeremiah 32-33/Hebrews 1

Focus scripture: Jeremiah 24:4-7/Titus 3:4-6

QUESTIONS

1. According to God, how is someone who incorrectly claims to be speaking for God a great hindrance to Him? How was the truth of prophecy proven (28:9)?

2. What was the great promise of a covenant, made in chapter 31? Why did God say there was a need for a new covenant?

3. Paul was concerned with how Christians appear to outsiders. What did he tell the following people to do so as to keep the image of Christianity bright before the world:

   a. elders

   b. older men

   c. older women

   d. young women

   e. young men

   f. slaves

4. In Paul's letter to Philemon about that man's runaway slave Onesimus, in what ways did Paul try to convince Philemon to welcome Onesimus back? How did Paul intend to follow up on his requests?

5. What could you generalize about the way God relates to people and/or human circumstances from any of this week's readings?

SCRIPTURES I WANT TO REMEMBER
AND ADDITIONAL NOTES

WEEK 45

Old Testament/ New Testament
- o   Day 1   Jeremiah 34-36/Hebrews 2
- o   Day 2   Jeremiah 37-39/Hebrews 3
- o   Day 3   Jeremiah 40-42/Hebrews 4
- o   Day 4   Jeremiah 43-45/Hebrews 5
- o   Day 5   Jeremiah 46-47/Hebrews 6
- o   Day 6   Jeremiah 48-49/Hebrews 7
- o   Day 7   Jeremiah 50/Hebrews 8

Focus scripture: Jeremiah 50:6-7/Hebrews 4:14-16

QUESTIONS

1. Why do you think that in Jeremiah 38:24-28, Jeremiah did not tell the officials the whole message he had delivered to the king? What would have been the reaction of the officials? Do you think this is characteristic of how people today often react to truth when it is unpleasant?

2. How did the remnant of Judah respond when Jeremiah told them not to go to Egypt? Why did they react this way? What was the result of their prideful disobedience?

3. Look at Hebrews 2:14-18 and 4:14-16. What qualifies Jesus to be able to understand and sympathize with our weaknesses? Because He loves us even when we are weak, how should we then feel when we go before God's throne in prayer?

4. What does Hebrews 6 say about the dangers of falling away from the truth? Did Paul believe that would happen to the people to whom he was writing? Why or why not?

5. What could you generalize about the way God relates to people and/or human circumstances from any of this week's readings?

SCRIPTURES I WANT TO REMEMBER
AND ADDITIONAL NOTES

WEEK 46

Old Testament / New Testament

- o   Day 1   Jeremiah 51-52/Hebrews 9
- o   Day 2   Lamentations 1-2/Hebrews 10:1-18
- o   Day 3   Lamentations 3-5/Hebrews 10:19-39
- o   Day 4   Ezekiel 1-2/Hebrews 11:1-19
- o   Day 5   Ezekiel 3-4/Hebrews 11:20-40
- o   Day 6   Ezekiel 5-7/Hebrews 12
- o   Day 7   Ezekiel 8-10/Hebrews 13

Focus scripture: Lamentations 3:22-26/Hebrews 11:1

QUESTIONS

1. In the book of Lamentations, whom does Jeremiah blame for the destruction that has come upon Jerusalem? Was the destruction deserved? How can catastrophe as great as this cause us to turn to God?

2. What does Ezekiel 3:16-21 say about the responsibility of those who see sin in the lives of others? Does it excuse a "live and let live" attitude for Christians?

3. Look at the example of the faithful men and women of the past listed in Hebrews 11. Are there examples there of people who understood fully why God had commanded them to do certain things? Do you think God requires men and women today to understand why we should obey His commands? How does our concept of God determine to a large degree how fully we will obey under trying circumstances?

4. Does Hebrews 12 teach that hardship and opposition in life are a sign of God's favor or disfavor? What is the ultimate result of such hardship?

5. What could you generalize about the way God relates to people and/or human circumstances from any of this week's readings?

SCRIPTURES I WANT TO REMEMBER
AND ADDITIONAL NOTES

WEEK 47

Old Testament/ New Testament

- o   Day 1   Ezekiel 11-13/James 1
- o   Day 2   Ezekiel 14-15/James 2
- o   Day 3   Ezekiel 16-17/James 3
- o   Day 4   Ezekiel 18-19/James 4
- o   Day 5   Ezekiel 20-21/James 5
- o   Day 6   Ezekiel 22-23/1 Peter I
- o   Day 7   Ezekiel 24-26/1 Peter 2

Focus scripture: Ezekiel 18:21-22/1 Peter 1:8-9

QUESTIONS

1. Why is it significant that the idolatry mentioned in Ezekiel 14 is in the heart? Why do you think the Lord would answer the idolatrous person in the way He said He'd answer? Does God lead men astray?

2. In chapters 16 and 23, how did the women defile themselves? Could they rightfully blame their pagan neighbors for their behavior? At whose hand were they punished?

3. What relationship did James say faith has to deeds? Would James accept either as valid alone? Why or why not? Why do you think James chose Abraham and Rahab as examples of working faith?

4. Both James and Peter (in 1 Peter) opened their epistles with statements about trials. What did each say? What would you tell a Christian brother or sister who is undergoing trials in his or her life which seem "unfair?" (See what Peter said in 1 Peter 2:19-20.)

5. What could you generalize about the way God relates to people and/or human circumstances from any of this week's readings?

SCRIPTURES I WANT TO REMEMBER
AND ADDITIONAL NOTES

WEEK 48

Old Testament/ New Testament

- o   Day 1   Ezekiel 27-29/1 Peter 3
- o   Day 2   Ezekiel 30-32/1 Peter 4
- o   Day 3   Ezekiel 33-34/1 Peter 5
- o   Day 4   Ezekiel 35-36/2 Peter 1
- o   Day 5   Ezekiel 37-39/2 Peter 2
- o   Day 6   Ezekiel 40-41/2 Peter 3
- o   Day 7   Ezekiel 42-44/1 John 1

Focus scripture: Ezekiel 36:22-28/1 John 1:5-7

QUESTIONS

1. A recurrent phrase (used 62 times in the book of Ezekiel) is "they shall know that I am the Lord." Find some of these references. By what means did God cause Israel to know that He was Lord? What does this tell you about Israel?

2. In chapter 34, whom does God blame for Israel's pitiful condition? What was their sin? How did God say in this chapter and in chapter 36 that He would make Israel know that He was the Lord?

3. What are the signs of a false teacher, as identified in 2 Peter?

4. What proofs did John give in 1 John chapter 1 that Jesus was the Christ?

5. What could you generalize about the way God relates to people and/or human circumstances from any of this week's readings?

SCRIPTURES I WANT TO REMEMBER
AND ADDITIONAL NOTES

WEEK 49

Old Testament/ New Testament

- o   Day 1   Ezekiel 45-46/1 John 2
- o   Day 2   Ezekiel 47-48/1 John 3
- o   Day 3   Daniel 1-2/1 John 4
- o   Day 4   Daniel 3-4/1 John 5
- o   Day 5   Daniel 5-7/2 John
- o   Day 6   Daniel 8-10/3 John
- o   Day 7   Daniel 11-12/Jude

Focus scripture: Daniel 3:16-18/1 John 3:18-24

QUESTIONS

1. What qualities did Daniel possess—besides being an able interpreter of dreams—that caused the king to make him a ruler in Babylon? How do you think the appointment of Daniel and his friends to power affected the rest of the Jews in captivity there?

2. One of the outstanding characteristics of Daniel's life was his devotion to prayer. Find examples of this and explain how prayer changed his situation in each case.

3. How do you reconcile John's statement that anyone who is born of
   God cannot continue sinning (1 John 3:6-9) with his prior
   statement to the effect that anyone who says that he does not sin
   is a liar (1 John 1:8-10)?

4. List the promises that John says can be ours in 1 John 5:13-20.

5. What could you generalize about the way God relates to people
   and/or human circumstances from any of this week's readings?

SCRIPTURES I WANT TO REMEMBER
AND ADDITIONAL NOTES

WEEK 50

Old Testament/ New Testament
- o   Day 1   Hosea 1-4/Revelation 1
- o   Day 2   Hosea 5-8/Revelation 2
- o   Day 3   Hosea 9-11/Revelation 3
- o   Day 4   Hosea 12-14/Revelation 4
- o   Day 5   Joel 1-3/Revelation 5
- o   Day 6   Amos 1-3/Revelation 6
- o   Day 7   Amos 4-6/Revelation 7

Focus scripture: Hosea 11:1-4/Revelation 3:19-22

QUESTIONS

1. In what ways was Israel's unfaithfulness to God a type of adultery?

2. In what ways had God tried to bring sinful people to their senses (Amos chapter 4)? In the past, how had other people responded? How had the Israelites to whom Amos was talking responded?

3. Look at the descriptions Jesus gave of the seven churches. Which one most closely resembles your own congregation? How can you begin to implement the reforms Jesus said were necessary?

4. Look at the descriptions of Jesus in Revelation 1 and 5. Which of His characteristics (as portrayed by symbolic descriptions) stand out most clearly in your mind?

5. What could you generalize about the way God relates to people and/or human circumstances from any of this week's readings?

SCRIPTURES I WANT TO REMEMBER
AND ADDITIONAL NOTES

WEEK 51

Old Testament/ New Testament

- o   Day 1   Amos 7-9/Revelation 8
- o   Day 2   Obadiah/Revelation 9
- o   Day 3   Jonah 1-4/Revelation 10
- o   Day 4   Micah 1-3/Revelation 11
- o   Day 5   Micah 4-5/Revelation 12
- o   Day 6   Micah 6-7/Revelation 13
- o   Day 7   Nahum 1-3/Revelation 14

Focus scripture: Micah 3:5-8/Revelation 12:7-9

QUESTIONS

1. God has often relented, or changed His mind, about destruction when His prophets begged Him to reconsider. Can you find examples of this in the writings of Amos and Jonah? Do you remember any other times in our prior readings that God relented from the destruction of individuals or nations? Why do you think in those cases He relented?

2. How did Jonah react when God told him to go to Ninevah? How did he react when Ninevah was spared? Contrast his actions with those of the Ninevites when they heard the word of the Lord.

3. John was told in the Revelation to eat a book. Can you remember
    from previous readings in the Old Testament what other prophet
    was told to eat a book? To measure the temple? Which other
    prophet wrote of Michael?

4. Look at the descriptions of Satan in Revelation 12 and list the
    characteristics you see portrayed there.

5. What could you generalize about the way God relates to people
    and/or human circumstances from any of this week's readings?

SCRIPTURES I WANT TO REMEMBER
AND ADDITIONAL NOTES

WEEK 52

Old Testament/ New Testament

- o   Day 1   Habakkuk 1-3/Revelation 15
- o   Day 2   Zephaniah 1-3/Revelation 16
- o   Day 3   Haggai 1-2/Revelation 17
- o   Day 4   Zechariah 1-6/Revelation 18
- o   Day 5   Zechariah 7-12/Revelation 19
- o   Day 6   Zechariah 13-14/Revelation 20
- o   Day 7   Malachi 1-4/Revelation 21-22

Focus scripture: Zephaniah 3:14-17/Revelation 21:3-4

QUESTIONS

1. In Haggai, the Lord revealed that the people's poverty was due to neglect of His house. What is His "house" today? What is the result of neglecting this house?

2. Malachi is like a "last will and testament"--the final word of God before a 400-year silence. What were the important messages of this book? Are they applicable today?

3. Look at the hymns sung to God in Revelation chapters 15-22. What characteristics of God did they praise? Pray now, together, praising God for these wonderful aspects of His character.

4. What could you generalize about the way that God relates to people and/or human circumstances from any of this week's readings?

SCRIPTURES I WANT TO REMEMBER
AND ADDITIONAL NOTES

Congratulations on your completion of reading God's Word! And won't it be grand to live in the heaven described in Revelation chapters 21 and 22! See you there!

Made in the USA
Coppell, TX
02 June 2020

26883950R00122